250 WORLD WAR II FACTS FOR KIDS

INTERESTING EVENTS & HISTORY
INFORMATION TO WIN TRIVIA

SCOTT MATTHEWS

CONTENTS

About The Author   v
7 Benefits Of Reading Facts   vi

WWII Facts   1
Also By Scott Matthews   63
Bonus: 3666 Interesting, Fun And Crazy Facts You Won't Believe Are True   64

Copyright © 2016 Scott Matthews

All rights reserved. No part of this publication may be reproduced, distributed or transmitted in any form or by any means, including photocopying, recording, or other electronic or mechanical methods, without the prior written permission of the publisher, except in the case of brief quotations embodied in critical reviews and certain other non-commercial uses permitted by copyright law.

Trademarked names appear throughout this book. Rather than use a trademark symbol with every occurrence of a trademarked name, names are used in an editorial fashion, with no intention of infringement of the respective owner's trademark. The information in this book is distributed on an "as is" basis, without warranty. Although every precaution has been taken in the preparation of this work, neither the author nor the publisher shall have any liability to any person or entity with respect to any loss or damage caused or alleged to be caused directly or indirectly by the information contained in this book.

ABOUT THE AUTHOR

Scott Matthews is a geologist, world traveller and author of the 'Amazing World Facts' series! He was born in Brooklyn New York by immigrant parents from the Ukraine but grew up in North Carolina. Scott studied at Duke University where he graduated with a degree in Geology and History.

His studies allowed him to travel the globe where he saw and learned amazing trivial knowledge with his many encounters. With the vast amount of interesting information he accumulated he created his best selling books 'Random, Interesting & Fun Facts You Need To Know'.

He hopes this book will provide you with hours of fun, knowledge, entertainment and laughter.

If you gain any knowledge from this book, think it's fun and could put a smile on someone's face, he would greatly appreciate your review on Amazon.

7 BENEFITS OF READING FACTS

1. Knowledge
2. Stress Reduction
3. Mental Stimulation
4. Better Writing Skills
5. Vocabulary Expansion
6. Memory Improvement
7. Stronger Analytical Thinking Skills

In the midst of chaos, there is also opportunity.

— Sun Tzu

WWII Timeline

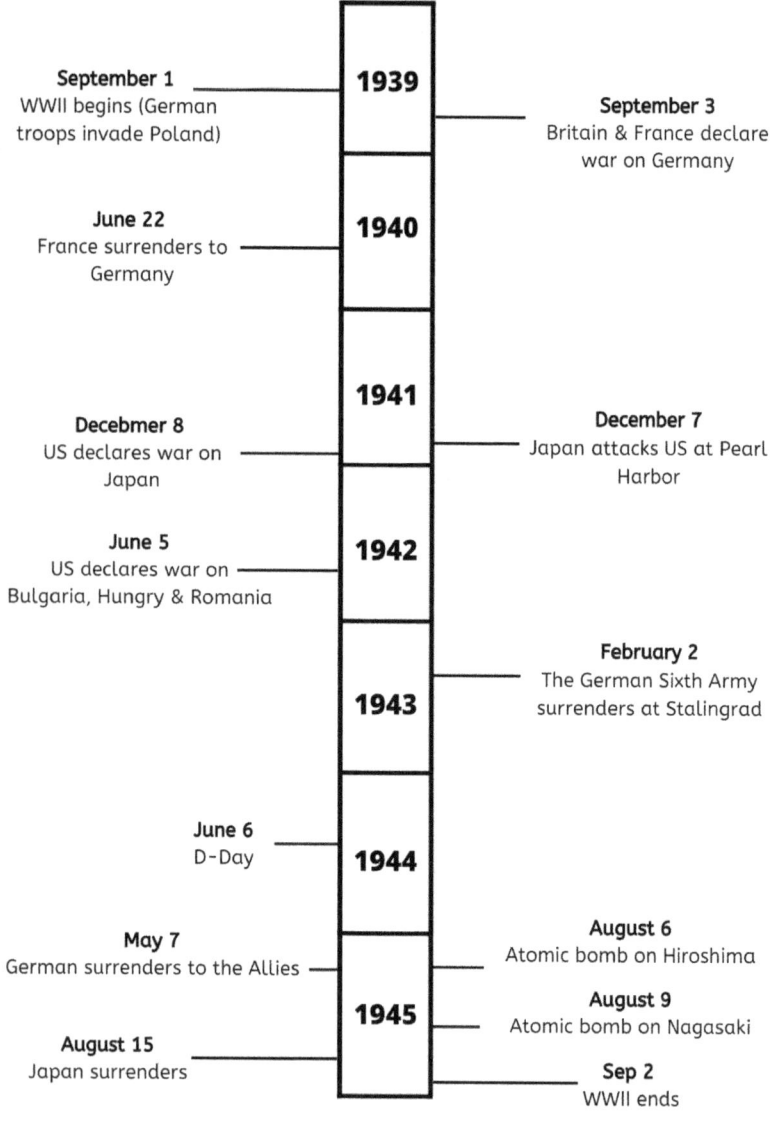

WWII FACTS

1) Throughout the 1930s, in the lead up to WWII, Nazi Germany engaged in a quick process of rearmament (building up of military resources) in violation of the conditions outlined in the Treaty of Versailles that ended WWI, and several other agreements. They also formed alliances with like-minded countries (e.g. Japan and Italy) and were getting ready for war.

2) In the lead up to WWII, France and Britain were trying their best to avoid another European war, so, as it became increasingly clear that Germany was hoping for war, the two allies remained committed to their policy of appeasement (going out of their way to avoid confrontation). There were some in France and Britain who wanted the allies to take the Nazi German threat more seriously, but the official position was to try to avoid doing anything that could anger the Germans and start a war.

3) WWII is officially considered to have started on September 1, 1939. The starting date of WWII is however

not universally agreed upon. Some historians argue that WWII started with the Second Sino-Japanese war (in July 1937) when war broke out between Japanese Imperialists and Chinese Revolutionaries at the Marco Polo Bridge. Others even believe that the war started way back in September 1931 when Japan invaded Manchuria.

4) On the 23rd of August, 1939, Germany and the Soviet Union signed a pact that clearly stated which Eastern and Central European countries fell within either of their spheres of influence. That pact cleared the way for German's invasion of Poland. Since Poland fell within Germany's sphere of influence according to the pact, it meant that the Soviets wouldn't intervene after Germany invaded the country. On September 1st, 1939, the Nazis invaded Poland.

5) Britain had promised to guarantee Poland's sovereignty (right to be a free country) after Hitler took over Czechoslovakia and people were worried that he would do the same with other small European countries. When the Nazis invaded Poland, Britain weighed its options, and two days later, on September 3rd 1939, they declared war on Germany.

6) The London air was filled with the sound of sirens minutes after British Prime Minister Neville Chamberlain finished his War Declaration speech. The sirens were meant to warn British citizens to take shelter in case German air raids were incoming.

7) The German invasion of Poland in September and October of 1939 resulted in the loss of many Polish lives.

70,000 polish fighters were killed and 133,000 injured. An estimated 45,000 civilians were killed in cold blood during the initial invasion and 700,000 citizens were taken as POW (prisoners of war).

German troops parade through Warsaw

8) The Soviet Union invaded Poland sixteen days after Germany did the same. The battle that followed led to the loss of 50,000 Polish lives. The USSR went into Poland under the alleged reason that the Polish State did not exist anymore, so its territory was up for grabs.

9) After declaring war on Germany, in September 1939, Britain adopted a non-aggression strategy. It involved the use of propaganda material in an attempt to influence public opinion in Germany. The Royal Air Force would drop leaflets in Germany, urging people to resist Nazi policies. Britain also hoped that by dropping pamphlets deep into German airspace, the Nazis would see how easy it would be for Britain to bomb them, and that would serve as a warning.

10) The Soviets tried to invade Finland between

November and December 1939. Their troops were however defeated, and the USSR was thrown out of the League of Nations. The Soviets made a second attempt to invade Finland in March of 1940, and this time they managed to get the Finns to sign a peace treaty with them, giving them control over some areas in Finland.

11) Germans used military tactics popularly known as Blitzkrieg. They involved the use of armoured trucks and aircraft to rapidly move deep into enemy territory. That way, they would manage to gain control over vast areas even before the opposing army had time to strategize and mount a proper defence.

12) In the wake of WWI, France had constructed the Maginot Line. This was a special wall that was lined with heavy weaponry, and manned by soldiers around the clock. It was made to protect France from the Germans. However, when Germany invaded France during WWII, they chose to avoid the Maginot Line altogether, and instead, they came in through the Ardennes (in Luxembourg and Belgium). The French didn't build a fortified wall in that area because they assumed that the Germans would try to avoid the harsh landscape of the Ardennes. Germans were able to stream into France in large numbers after they broke through French defences in The Battle of Sedan (which was fought between 12-15 May in 1940). That was the beginning of the fall of France.

13) WWII ended on September 2nd, 1945. It lasted a total of 6 years and 1 day.

14) WWII was fought in Europe, the Pacific Ocean, the

Atlantic Ocean, China, South East Asia, The Middle East, the Mediterranean, Australia, The North and the Horn of Africa, and briefly, in North and South America. It was fought between the Allied Powers and the Axis Powers. The Allied Powers included the Soviet Union, the United States, the United Kingdom, and China. The Axis Powers included Germany, The Japanese Empire, and the Italians.

15) WWII was fought under a state of "total war" (where the entire economy of a participating country is directed towards the war effort), and it involved more than thirty countries and 100 million combatants.

16) WWII is still the deadliest conflict in all of human history. It is estimated that between seventy million and eighty five million lives were lost during the conflict. The war included the holocaust, the use of nuclear weapons, the strategic use of starvation and disease to weaken entire countries, and the bombings of civilian populations.

17) Nationalists in Germany were unhappy with the treaty of Versailles (signed after WWI) where Germany lost a lot of territory and colonies and were forced to make financial restitution. This led to widespread anger and resentment in the country, which led to the rise of nationalist leaders like Hitler, who was Chancellor of Germany during WWII.

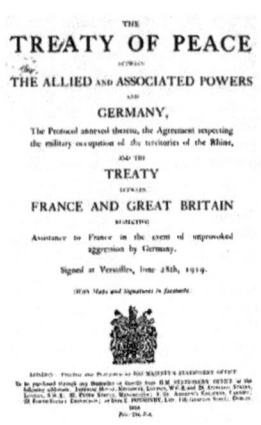

Treaty of Versailles

18) The League of Nations, which was in charge of keeping the peace between countries after WWI and before WWII, turned out to be a very weak organization. Countries would openly violate League of Nations rules without suffering any consequences. When the League of Nations tried to intervene in conflicts, some countries would just leave the organization. Japan left when the League of Nations spoke up against its decision to invade China.

19) Coming out of WWI, Italy was unhappy that Britain and France had not honored the promises they had made during the peace settlement. At the same time, fascism was on the rise in Italy, and that paved the way for Benito Mussolini who seized power and became the Italian leader, and Hitler's close ally during WWII. Leading up to WWII, Italy wanted to be a world power, and it pursued an aggressive foreign policy with the intention of creating a "New Roman Empire." Italy had always wanted to have Ethiopia as a colony. It invaded Ethiopia, and that resulted

in a war that lasted between 1935 and 1936. France and Britain did nothing to stop this invasion, even though it was a clear violation of the rules outlined by the League of Nations. This made Italy bold and more willing to violate other international laws.

20) Right before WWII, European powers were involved in a proxy war (a competition to see which country was more powerful) during the Spanish Civil War. Germany and Italy backed the nationalists in Spain, who were led by General Francisco Franco. The nationalists won. The USSR backed the existing Spanish Government which lost the Civil War. European powers used the Spanish Civil war to test out some of their new military technologies and strategies, which they ended up using during WWII.

21) The first official battle of WWII was the Battle of WesterPlatte, which was fought near the Polish Border with Germany.

22) When Poland fell, the Polish army surrendered to Germany in October of 1939, but the Polish government never did. Polish government officials fled the country and formed a "government in exile", which worked secretly with the allies in an attempt to regain control of Poland. That same month, the Western part of Poland was annexed by Germany, and the Eastern part was annexed by the Soviet Union. Some Polish territories were handed to Slovakia and Lithuania.

23) In 1939, Lithuania, Latvia, Estonia, and Finland were determined to be within the Soviet Union's sphere of

influence. The USSR ordered these countries to allow its troops to be stationed within their borders. All countries agreed, except Finland, and this led to the Finno-Soviet War.

24) Germany brought in a lot of iron ore from Sweden during WWII. In fact, it invaded both Norway and Denmark in 1940, just to protect its supply route from Sweden.

25) The British public was unhappy with Neville Chamberlain's leadership (especially after the Germans won control over Norway). As a result, Winston Churchill was appointed Prime Minister on May 10, 1940.

Winston Churchill as Prime Minister

26) Paris fell on the 14th of June, 1940. Italy had declared war on both Britain and France and it had invaded France on the 10th June, 1940. The French army was overwhelmed fighting both Germany and Italy, and that led to the fall of Paris. France signed a peace agreement with

Germany on the 22nd June, 1940. Under that agreement, France was occupied by both Germany and Italy. There was an area in France (the Vichy State) that was unoccupied by Axis forces, but it couldn't stand up against Germany, so it fell under their control.

27) After France fell, Britain tried to destroy French military equipment and resources to keep them from the hands of the German Military.

28) America had passed the Neutrality Act that was meant to keep it from joining any armed conflict in Europe, but in November, 1939, it revised the Act and started to sell arms and other resources to the allies. To maintain the appearance of neutrality, the United States would let countries ship their own weapons across the Atlantic Ocean to Europe.

29) The Axis powers (Germany, Italy, and Japan) signed the Tripartite Pact in September, 1940. Under this pact, any country (with the exception of the Soviet Union) that would enter into war with one of the three countries, would effectively be at war with all of them. Slovakia, Hungary, and Romania joined the Axis powers in November, 1940, while Bulgaria and Yugoslavia joined later on in March, 1941. Yugoslavian opposition overthrew the government and opposed the decision to join the axis power, but Hitler invaded both Yugoslavia and Greece at the same time. By the end of May, 1941, all Balkan States were under the control of the Axis powers.

30) The Soviet Union considered joining the Axis powers in 1940, and they were in negotiations with Germany to

do so, but they couldn't agree on the terms. The soviets had many demands that threatened Germany's authority as the leader of the Axis Powers, so Hitler decided to invade the Soviets instead of making them allies.

31) WWII caused one of the most serious refugee crises in history. In the summer of 1940 alone, eight million Belgian, Dutch and French people were displaced from their homes, with nowhere to go.

32) In mid-1940, the British Royal Air force had 1,960 aircraft, while the German air force (the Luftwaffe) had over 2,500 aircrafts (including fighters, bombers, dive-bombers, coastal planes, and recon planes). This meant that by sheer numbers alone, the Germans had a stronger air force than the British during the early stages of WWII.

Royal Air Force Operation in the Far East

33) In 1940, the German air force bombed cities in Britain (mostly London) and it led to the loss of 40,000 civilian lives. This was known as the Blitz. London, in particular, was bombed continuously for fifty seven nights, starting September 7th, 1940. More than 180,000 people spent

their nights in underground shelters (mostly tunnels) in London.

34) The famous "Keep Calm and Carry On" posters were first issued by the British government in 1939 as the country prepared for WWII. It was one of a series of posters that were issued to cheer up and reassure the public who were worried about possible German air raids.

35) After the Germans bombarded British cities, there was rubble all over the British streets. The Government collected all that rubble and used it to construct runways for the Royal Air force. This showed that despite the grim circumstances, Britain had not lost its fighting spirit, and was willing to make the best of a bad situation.

36) The allied powers and axis powers fought hard for control of the Mediterranean. Between January and August of 1941 alone, ninety axis ships were sunk in the Mediterranean.

37) Hitler approved the euthanasia program in Germany to get rid of people who were seen as burdens to society. As a result, 100,000 Germans with physical disabilities or mental illnesses were murdered by August, 1941.

38) Control of oil supplies was very crucial during WWII. Both sides put a lot of effort into acquiring or keeping oil-rich territories. British and Soviet troops invaded Iran to take over its oil resources while German and Italian forces fought hard to retain control over Romanian oil fields.

39) In 1925, fourteen years before WWII, Adolf Hitler published a book (Mein Kampf) in which he expressed his

intention to invade other countries and put them under German control. Long before WWII, the Nazi leader already believed that war was necessary to secure the future wealth of Germany.

40) The Nazis used hunger as a war strategy. Under the "Nazi Hunger Plan", more than two million soviet prisoners were literally starved to death in 1941.

41) After the Germans took over Poland, they rounded up all mentally handicapped Polish citizens, and in November, 1939, they used chambers filled with carbon dioxide to kill all of them.

42) When the Nazis rounded up and detained or murdered Jews and people of other ethnicities, they would take their possessions and reuse them. Valuable items would be given to soldiers as gifts, clothes would be given to Germans who needed them, and metallic items would be used as raw material to make weapons.

43) An estimated total of six million Jews were killed in the holocaust during WWII. It's estimated that about two million Jews living in the Western Soviet Union were murdered and buried in mass graves between 1941 and 1944, in what was known as the "holocaust by bullets."

The holocaust in Poland

44) Otto Kretschmer, a German Naval commander, is considered the most prolific submariner of WWII. He was responsible for sinking thirty seven allied ships. He was captured by the British royal navy in March of 1941.

45) As WWII went on, Americans wanted to lend material support to the allies without really joining the war. As a result, the Senate passed a Lend-Lease Bill which allowed the United States to loan war machinery and supplies to the allies, which they would pay back after the war.

46) 60% of all Japanese soldiers who died during WWII lost their lives due to malnutrition and resultant diseases.

47) The Americans bombed Iwo Jima Island for seventy six days before they sent in an assault fleet of about 30,000 marines to invade the island.

48) The US, Britain, and several other Western nations put an oil embargo (restriction) on Japan after it invaded Indo-China in July, 1941. This greatly limited Japan's military capabilities. Japan was planning to invade the Soviet Union from the East, but it put off those plans because of the oil restriction.

49) Japan's WWII strategy involved grabbing all European colonies in Asia so that they could exploit resources from those colonies and use the land as a defensive perimeter, creating some distance between their homeland and the nearest European armies. Throughout the war, Japan planned to neutralize America's fleet in the pacific because it wanted to be the sole power in the Asia-pacific region.

50) When the US, UK, Australia, and China declared war on Japan, the Soviet Union (even though it was one of the allies) still maintained a neutrality agreement that it had in place with Japan.

51) On the 1st of January, 1942, the main allies, together with twenty two other governments (including some governments in exile) agreed to implement the Atlantic Charter. The countries agreed that none of them would sign a separate peace deal with the Axis powers. This ensured that the allies weren't weakened by some countries leaving the war before they had totally won (like Russia did in WWI).

52) Even though all allied powers agreed that defeating Germany was their biggest priority, they had different preferences when it came to strategy. For example, in 1942, the Americans thought that a direct large scale attack through France would be the best approach. The British wanted a war of attrition (where they would attack Germany on the outer edges of their territory, and wear them out over time). The Soviets thought that starting a second front would strain German resources (at this point, they were the only ones fighting Germans on land at the Eastern front).

53) Japan was able to conquer many Asian and pacific territories by May, 1942. With the help of Thailand, they conquered Malaya, the Dutch East Indies, Burma, Rabaul, and Singapore. They were also able to capture the Philippine Commonwealth, despite tough resistance from America and Filipino soldiers. Japan had many easy victories over countries and territories that weren't prepared for war. As a result, they became overconfident, and they over-extended their army, making them vulnerable.

54) The ability to intercept enemy messages and to break their code was an important part of WWII. It determined the outcomes of many battles, for example, Americans broke Japanese naval codes, and as a result, they were able to win the Midway Battle (it was called the Midway Battle because it was in the pacific, halfway between America and Japan).

Battle of Midway- An unexpected victory

55) Four out of five German soldiers who lost their lives

during WWII, died in the Eastern Front, fighting the Soviets.

56) Before the swastika was a symbol for Nazi Germany, it used to be an ancient symbol for good fortune and fertility in several Eastern religious traditions (including Hinduism and Buddhism).

57) In response to Hitler's treatment of Jews in Europe, more than 600,000 American Jews joined the US armed forces and fought in WWII.

58) For the entire duration of the war, the allies dropped over 3.4 million tons of bombs. That's roughly 27,700 tons every single month for six continuous years.

59) The Japanese "Kamikaze" war strategy was created as a way to balance out America's technological advantage during WWII. It involved filling planes with explosives and letting pilots fly them on a suicide mission into American military establishments. An estimated three thousand Japanese pilots took part in the Kamikaze attacks.

60) Japan used "wind ship weapons" to target America. They launched about 9,000 balloons that carried bombs, and sent them to different destinations in America. This mission generally failed because only a thousand balloons hit their targets, and only six people died as a result of the attack.

61) It's estimated that 1.5 million children were killed in the holocaust. The vast majority of them were Jewish children, but tens of thousands of Gypsy children were also murdered.

62) The USSR had the highest number of casualties in WWII. It's estimated that it lost twenty one million people in total.

63) The concentration camps were so bad that even after the Jewish detainees were liberated from these camps, thousands of them died later on as a result of the conditions they were subjected to in the camps. Between the Bergen-Belsen and Dachau camps, more than 15,000 detainees died within six weeks after being liberated.

64) The Nazis created a fictional person named Max Heiliger. They used his identity to open bank accounts that they used to launder the money and gold they had stolen from the Jews that were detained.

65) Before WWII, Europe had been the center of world power for centuries. After the war, European powers declined, and the US and USSR emerged as superpowers.

66) Radar was used for the first time by aviators in WWII. It was accidentally invented before the war by a British engineer who was trying to create a "death ray" to destroy enemy planes.

67) When British soldiers liberated the Bergen-Belsen camp in April, 1945, they had to burn it to the ground to contain the spread of typhus.

68) During WWII, American factories manufactured seven million rifles, three million machine guns, 650,000 jeeps, 300,000 aircraft, and 89,000 tanks. They were used by Americans as well as allied forces to win the war.

Military production during World War II

69) The Nazis performed lots of brutal medical experiments on Jewish detainees during WWII. In the name of research, they conducted several inhumane things including: hitting people's skulls with hammers to see how much pressure it would take for skulls to crack, repeatedly breaking people's bones to see if the healing process would stop after several breaks, exposing men and women's reproductive organs to X-rays to see how different doses affected their ability to conceive or bear children, and amputating people to perform transplant experiments. The Nazis kept detailed records of their experiments, but today, it's considered unethical to use any of that material for reference purposes.

70) On January 20, 1942, at the Wannsee Conference in Berlin, Germany decided to implement the "Final Solution" that was proposed by a group led by Heinrich Himmler. The Jewish community was seen as a "problem" in Germany and some other fascist countries at the time,

and the final solution meant the "extermination" of all Jews within German territory.

71) The bloodiest battle of WWII was the Battle of Stalingrad. It's also considered by many historians to be the bloodiest battle in human history. It lasted from 1942 to 1943, and anywhere between 800,000 and 1.6 million lives were lost.

Battle of Stalingrad

72) American military spending rose dramatically during WWII. In 1940, when America was still neutral, it had a defence budget of $1.9 billion. However, by 1945, military spending had shot up to $59.8 billion.

73) The SS (Schutzstaffel) was a powerful paramilitary organization in Germany during WWII. They started out as Hitler's personal guards, but they became the most influential and most feared group in all of Nazi Germany.

74) A German physicist named Hermann Oberth had the idea to build a space weapon for the Nazis. The concept

involved putting a giant magnifying glass (which he referred to as the "sun-gun") in space and using it to concentrate the sun's beams and target them at important British and allied installations.

75) The Germans murdered Poles by the millions, but in the process, they noticed that Polish babies looked very similar to German babies. They decided to kidnap around 50,000 Polish babies and give them to German families so that they could be "Germanized."

76) The US military wanted to minimize its use of atomic bombs, but it already had several potential targets lined up. Had Japan not surrendered, Tokyo would have been the next city in Japan to be hit by an atomic bomb.

77) Germany had the strongest artillery gun of any nation that fought in the war. The artillery gun was named Karl, and it had the ability to shoot shells of up to 2.5 tons over a distance of three miles (five kilometers) and could burst through up to nine feet (three meters) of concrete. Karl was mostly used in wars against the USSR.

78) Adolf Hitler had a nephew named William Hitler who was an American citizen and served in the US Navy during the war. William Hitler changed his name after the war.

79) Germany was the first country to use jet fighters in WWII. Unfortunately for them, the jet fighters were made too late in the game to change the final outcome of the war.

80) Thousands of people in German-occupied territories

risked their lives to save their Jewish friends and neighbors from the Nazis. Denmark managed to save its entire Jewish population. People like Oscar Schindler, Raoul Wallenberg, and Chiune Sugihara were in good standing with the Nazis, but still put their lives on the line to save as many Jews as they could.

81) During the Pearl Harbor attack, 2,402 Americans were killed, and another 1,280 were wounded. Eighteen out of ninety-six ships anchored at the harbor, and three hundred aircraft were either damaged, destroyed, or sunk.

82) When Germany was defeated, many of the most-wanted war criminals (mostly high ranking Nazi officers) hid in displaced person camps and pretended to be refugees. Many of them managed to get away and they were never brought to justice.

83) Japan had a large spy ring in North America during WWII. Contrary to popular belief, most Japanese spies were located in Mexico, not in the United States. They were mostly tasked with spying on America's Atlantic Fleet.

84) Eighty five percent of all POWs in Soviet camps ended up dying in the camps.

85) Some people in occupied European countries collaborated with the Nazis, either willingly or as a result of coercion. When these countries were liberated, some collaborators were shot or beaten by angry locals, and some female collaborators had their heads forcefully shaved.

86) The British military used balloons to protect population centers during air raids. The balloons were linked to networks of steel cables before they were left to drift upwards. This forced German bombers to fly higher to avoid the cables, and as a result, they were more likely to miss their targets.

87) After the Pearl Harbor raid, President Theodore Roosevelt realized that he needed a bulletproof car. At the time, the US Government had a $750 cap on how much taxpayers' money could be spent on a car. The president had to use an armoured limousine that the treasury department had seized from notorious gangster Al Capone.

88) Nazis would identify themselves to each other with their "Heil Hitler" salute during WWII. Those who refused to do the salute were considered enemies of Germany.

89) During the blitzkrieg raids, German planes were fitted with sirens that sounded like loud screams. This was meant to terrify and psychologically torture the civilians in the targeted cities.

Strategic bombing during World War II

90) In 1938, the year before the start of WWII, Hitler was Time Magazine's Man of the year.

91) A twelve-year-old boy named Calvin Graham joined the US Navy. He was so brave in his service to the Navy that he was awarded a Purple Heart and a Bronze Star. The Navy only found out that he was a minor after the honors were already awarded.

92) Germany never actually declared war on any of the countries it invaded in Europe or Asia. In fact, the US is the only country on which Germany formally declared war during WWII.

93) Hitler believed that he was forming the third German Empire, also known as the "Third Reich." According to him, the Holy Roman Empire (of 962 to 1806) was the First Reich, the German Empire (of 1871 to 1918) was the Second Reich, and his Nazi Empire was therefore the Third Reich.

94) A Yugoslavian spy named Dusko Popov was able to get

information that Japan planned to attack Pearl Harbor. He shared this information with the American government, but the FBI didn't take his warning seriously.

95) Two hundred Navajo Native Americans were enlisted in the US Marines as "code talkers" during WWII. They used the Navajo language as the basis for their code, and the Japanese weren't able to crack the code at all for the duration of the war.

96) All European and world powers had access to chemical weapons during WWII, but only Japan and Italy used such weapons in battle.

97) The SS (Schutzstaffel: a major paramilitary organization under Adolf Hitler and the Nazi Party in Nazi Germany) executed all of Hitler's political opponents and anyone within Germany who spoke out against Hitler's actions or objected to inhumane orders. They executed eighty four generals on suspicion that they were plotting against Hitler. Even though Hitler was democratically elected, he turned into a dictator, and he wouldn't allow any real political opposition in Germany during WWII.

98) The allied forces lost more than 20,000 aircrafts during WWII. The US Army Air Force (the predecessor to the US Air Force) lost 9,949 aircrafts, while the Royal Air Force lost 11,965 aircrafts.

99) After attempting and failing to develop nuclear weapons, the Nazis built a dirty bomb which they intended to transport across the Pacific on a submarine, and to detonate it on the American West Coast. The uranium for the dirty bomb was lost on its way to Japan,

and many have speculated that it was seized by the Americans and used to make the bombs that were dropped on Hiroshima and Nagasaki.

100) Nazi scientists developed effective biological weapons during WWII, but Hitler wouldn't allow such weapons to be used in battle. Some historians believe that he personally had bad experiences with such weapons as a soldier in WWI, so he didn't want them out there. Biological weapons were just as likely to kill the German soldiers using them, as they were to kill enemy soldiers.

101) Queen Elizabeth served as a mechanic and a driver during WWII. Even though she was just a teenager, she served in the Auxiliary Territorial Service, repairing engines for a fleet of military vehicles.

Princess Elizabeth Undergoing Instruction at the Auxiliary Territorial Service Training Centre (Front row, sitting between the two dogs)

102) An American Soldier named John McKinney single-

handedly fought off a hundred Japanese soldiers. McKinney was standing guard at a military establishment in the Philippines when Japanese soldiers stormed the place. He fought off and killed a total of thirty eight attackers, first with gunfire, then with his bare hands. He was awarded the Medal of Honor.

103) Japanese scientists tried to develop a death ray that could kill people from several miles away. However, their first model was a failure. It could only kill its target from half a mile (800 meters) away, provided that the target didn't move for ten whole minutes. The Japanese eventually decided to abandon that project.

104) Adolf Hitler had a private train that was codenamed "Amerika", an odd choice given the fact that the US was his adversary during WWII. The train served as his mobile home and office whenever he would travel around Germany or visit occupied territories. The train's name was changed after America joined the war.

105) The Nazis came very close to acquiring large amounts of plutonium during WWII. When the Germans went into Norway, they took over a factory that produced heavy water (a liquid that is used in nuclear reactors) which they could use to produce plutonium. However, a special team of Norwegian soldiers destroyed the factory with explosives, so the Nazis weren't able to use it.

106) Throughout the war, Germany and Britain fought for control of the Atlantic Ocean in what was known as the Battle of the Atlantic. The Germans tried to sink all ships that supplied goods to Britain. On the other side, the

Royal Navies of Britain and Canada, and later the US Navy, fought off the Germans in a bid to protect merchant shipping lines.

107) Germany considered using potato beetles to destroy Britain's potato crop. The plan would involve dropping forty million beetles from German aircraft onto British potato fields. The Nazis were able to breed several million beetles, but they didn't manage to get to the forty million before the war ended. The idea was that by destroying the British food supply, they would weaken the whole country, and lower morale for the war.

108) The Soviet army trained over 2,000 women as snipers. Some of these women became the deadliest sharpshooters to ever grace the battlefield. A few were individually credited with killing hundreds of German soldiers.

Women in the Russian and Soviet military

109) The Buchenwald concentration camp was run by Master Sergeant Martin Sommer, a brutal Nazi who came

to be known as "Hangman of Buchenwald." Sommer would hang people by the wrists and let them wail in agony until they died.

110) In the earlier stages of WWII, Hitler had hoped that after invading and capturing France, Britain would sign a peace agreement and let him have control over most of Europe. At the time, the US and USSR were still neutral. Britain wouldn't agree to any of Hitler's conditions, and together with its dominions, it stood up to the Nazis until the other allies joined the fight.

111) Japan attacked Pearl Harbor on a Sunday because they knew that it was a day of rest in most Western countries (which were primarily Christian). They figured that Americans were more likely to be caught off-guard on a Sunday.

112) You've probably heard of Auschwitz before, but do you know just how many souls were taken in this camp? Auschwitz was the deadliest of all Nazi concentration camps during WWII. Over a million people had died in that camp by the end of the war. When the camp was fully operational, 6,000 people were killed there every single day. Of the 7,500 Nazis who worked at that camp, only 750 of them were punished after the war, and most of the others went free.

Auschwitz concentration camp

113) At the Dauchau Concentration Camp located in Southern Germany, Nazi officers would line up Soviet POWs and shoot them for target practice.

114) Operation Dynamo was one of the most daring large-scale operations of WWII. Over three hundred thousand British troops and 140,000 allied troops were rescued from behind enemy lines at Dunkirk Beach in France after the area fell under German control.

115) D-Day (June 6, 1944) was (and still remains) the largest, sea, land and air military operation in history. It was the beginning of the allied invasion of Europe. Over one hundred thousand amphibious troops landed on the Beaches of Normandy, and 20,000 paratroopers jumped into France (which was under German occupation at the time). The invasion of Normandy was led by General Dwight D. Eisenhower, who went on to become the President of the United States. To date, he remains one of the most revered military men in US history.

116) After the fall of Berlin, twenty-four top Nazi leaders were tried for war crimes during what came to be known as the Nuremberg Trials. At least half of them were sentenced to death.

117) Italian leader Benito Mussolini was executed on April 28, 1945, when the axis powers were about to fall.

118) Some Nazi commanders secretly negotiated the terms of surrender with the allied forces even before Berlin was captured. However, these negotiations were kept secret until after Hitler was dead.

119) The Japanese surrendered not just because of the atomic bombing of Hiroshima and Nagasaki, but also because the Soviets were finally planning to invade their territory, and they didn't have the manpower or resources to fight them back.

120) France was freed from Nazi occupation on August 25, 1944, by allied troops. Encouraged by news of the allied invasion, French fighters started resisting German control from within, and many German soldiers had actually fled Paris by the time allied troops got there.

121) The invasion of Normandy was the key turning point that led to victory for the allied forces. Four hundred and twenty five thousand combatants died during the invasion, but in the end, it led to the liberation of France and Belgium by the end of 1944.

122) Adolf Hitler committed suicide on April 30, 1945, while hiding in his bunker in Berlin. The USSR Red Army was closing in, and he didn't want to be captured.

123) Before the United States dropped atomic bombs on Japan, it air-dropped thousands of notices over more than thirty five Japanese cities, warning that the cities would soon be destroyed and that civilians should move out.

124) When Nazi soldiers came for the Jewish population in the Polish town of Rozwadow, two doctors created a fake typhus epidemic. The Nazis, who were afraid of contracting the disease, decided to keep away from the town. Eight thousand Jews were saved because of this act of trickery.

125) Before deciding to kill all Jewish people, the Nazis had considered deporting all of them to the island of Madagascar in the Indian Ocean. The Germans thought that the Jews would die of starvation in Madagascar because of the harsh conditions there. However, this plan was never put to action because the Germans figured out that it would just be easier to put the Jews in concentration camps.

126) Japan tried to start a bubonic plague outbreak in China by dropping fleas infected with the disease into a Chinese city. There were several outbreaks of the disease in the area, but the plague didn't happen on the scale that Japan had hoped for.

127) Some scholars have argued that WWII was a continuation of WWI with a long break in between. That's because most countries fought on the same side that they did in the previous war, and many of the conditions that led to WWII were a direct result of how WWI ended. The Germans annexed Austria and other countries because

they needed more land, labor, and other resources to pay their WWI reparation debts faster and build wealth for themselves.

128) Hitler's political party was called the National Socialist Party. Initially, it was abbreviated as "Naso." It later came to be known as the Nazi Party after a journalist named Konrad Heiden used the Bavarian word "Nazi" which meant "simple-minded" to make fun of Hitler and his followers.

Nazi Party

129) Hollywood movies helped shape Americans' understanding of the Nazis and the Japanese during the war. The movie studios were sympathetic to the Allies from the very beginning of the war, so they replaced gangster villains with Nazis, and they portrayed Japanese soldiers as inhumane and psychopathic.

130) The US and New Zealand tried to develop "tsunami bombs" during WWII. These were devices that were

meant to be detonated to create a thity-three-foot (ten meter) tsunami that would wash over entire cities that were located next to the beach. These weapons were tested in New Zealand, but they were never used in battle.

131) Hitler considered the fall of Paris and occupation of France as payback for France's victory during WWI. When France was about to surrender to the Nazi's during WWII, Hitler ordered the Nazis to tear down the Paris Museum where WWI memorabilia was displayed. On his orders, the railway cabins in which the Germans signed the WWI armistice were returned to the exact location where the event took place, as a way of undoing Germany's past failure and humiliating the French.

132) The London Zoo killed all snakes and other venomous animals during WWII because they were concerned that the zoo would be destroyed during air raids, and the animals would escape and harm people.

133) Whenever the allied forces captured high-ranking German officers, they would send them to live in a luxurious guarded building in Trent Park. The Nazi officers were treated well, but this was a plan to make them relax and lower their guard. It turns out that the building was wired with microphones, and British Intelligence Services listened to their conversations and learned a lot about what was going on in Berlin. For example, Britain learned that many Nazi officers actually thought Hitler was mad.

134) A Muslim cleric named Si Kaddour Benghabrit saved the lives of hundreds of Jews by hiding them in the Paris Grand Mosque and providing them with fake papers

to conceal their identities. Despite the widespread bitterness between Muslims and Jews at that time, the cleric was willing to set aside those differences to help save Jewish lives.

135) As the red army retreated during the German invasion of the Soviet Union, the soldiers would destroy most buildings that were suitable for use as command posts. They would then wire the few remaining suitable buildings with explosives and set them to detonate after a week or so. This way, they managed to kill high ranking German military officials and cripple Nazi operations.

136) One Japanese soldier named Hiroo Onoda never heard the news that Japan had surrendered after WWII. His entire unit was killed in battle, so he hid in the forest on an island in the Philippines. He held his position and waited for thirty years. When he was found in the forest in 1974, he wouldn't believe that Japan had lost the war. He refused to go back home, thinking it was all a trick, and they had to bring in his old commander to convince him that the war was over.

137) Three-quarters of all those who served in submarines during WWII were killed in battle by the end of the war.

138) From the time America entered WWII to the time the war ended, the manufacture of civilian cars came to a standstill. While three million cars were made in 1941, only 139 cars were made between 1942 and the end of the war in mid-1945. All car makers were focused on manufacturing military vehicles.

139) A polish midwife named Stanislawa Leszczynska

delivered over 3,000 newborn babies in Auschwitz. Only twenty five of those children survived by the time the concentration camp was liberated.

140) Henry Ford and Adolf Hitler mutually admired each other. They both had pictures of each other on their desks. Although Henry Ford still remains one of the greatest American industrialists of all time, his views on Hitler and white supremacy left a dark mark on his legacy.

141) Hitler told his generals to collect thousands of Jewish artefacts so that when Germany won the war and succeeded in killing all Jews, he would create a "Museum of an Extinct Race."

142) A Spanish double agent named Joan Pujol Garcia worked for Britain and Germany at the same time during WWII. He was given medals in both countries for his distinguished service.

143) Russia and Japan never signed a peace treaty after WWII. That means that the two countries never officially acknowledged that the war was over between them. At least on paper, the two countries are still technically at war even today.

144) After Hitler invaded the Soviet Union, he told the Nazis that he wanted them to kill everyone in Moscow and then turn the entire city into an artificial lake.

145) The allies created a plan to make Hitler less aggressive by adding oestrogen (the female sex hormone) to his food supply. They had first considered poisoning Hitler, but they decided against it because he had food tasters.

Oestrogen, on the other hand, was a tasteless chemical, and its effects would be delayed, so no one would suspect anything was wrong. The plan was cancelled because British assets in Berlin were too afraid to carry it out.

146) German soldiers who fought in WWII were given large amounts of methamphetamine. At the time, it was believed that the drug could keep soldiers alert and increase their endurance on the battlefield.

147) After leading Britain into victory during WWII, Prime Minister Winston Churchill was voted out of office in the middle of ongoing peace conferences.

148) The British military used special searchlights called "Moonlight Batteries" to create artificial moonlight that was used to guide troop movements during the war.

149) A Flight Sergeant named Nicholas Alkemade fell 18,000 feet (5.5 kilometers) without a parachute when his aircraft was destroyed by enemy fire. He miraculously survived, and his only injury was a sprained leg.

150) When allied troops landed on Normandy Beach, they opened a second front in the land war against Germany. Up to that point, Germany had only been fighting on the Eastern front (against the Soviets), so for the first time, they had to divide their land troops into two, which weakened them significantly.

151) The BBC (British Broadcasting Corporation) was involved in the planning stages before D-Day. The British military used the media organization to run a contest where people would send in holiday photos taken at

French beaches and the person with the best photo would win. The photos were collected and analysed, so that the allies could figure out which areas were suitable for an amphibious landing. Over 7,000 ships were used in the landing of Normandy. British Prime Minister Winston Churchill wanted to go to sea and watch the landing first hand, but several generals advised him against it. He only backed down when King George VI said that if Churchill went to the battlefront, he too would come along.

Operation Overlord

152) The allies used deception campaigns (mostly spreading false rumors) to keep the Germans guessing on where exactly they planned to land when they invaded France. As a result, Germany had to split its troops to cover different beaches, which made them vulnerable.

153) The phrase "loose lips sink ships" was coined during WWII. There was concern that German spies were all over Britain, and if anyone talked carelessly about the war,

they could accidentally leak information to the spies and it could result in the loss of life.

154) The phrase "loose lips sink ships" was coined during WWII. There was concern that German spies were all over Britain, and if anyone talked carelessly about the war, they could accidentally leak information to the spies and it could result in the loss of life.

155) After America joined WWII, General George Patton was considered the best general that the allied forces had. The Germans were aware of this fact. In the lead up to D-Day, the allies used General Patton to trick the Germans into thinking they intended to land at Kent instead of Normandy. They built some dummy equipment near Kent, and they made sure that General Patton was spotted by German informants on his way to Kent. The trick worked so well, that even after the landing of Normandy, the Germans still kept some of their best troops at Kent, expecting a second landing.

156) D-day was an international effort with fighters from many different countries, so the allied forces had to overcome lots of cultural differences, language barriers, and issues that arose from unclear chains of command, to make the invasion work. Most fighters were American, British and Canadian, but there were also fighters from Australia, Belgium, France, Greece, Norway, Rhodesia, Poland, Holland, and Czech.

157) British scientists designed a "life pod" to protect Prime Minister Winston Churchill during high altitude flights. Churchill's doctors were concerned that a man of

his age could die during such flights because airplane cabins weren't properly pressurized back then. The life pod was too big to fit in the plane, so Churchill never actually used it.

158) The Germans developed the 88mm anti-tank and anti-aircraft artillery gun. It was widely used in the Soviet and North African theaters of war, and it was one of the most feared weapons of the entire war. The artillery gun could fire 17-pound (7kg) grenades, which could go up to several thousand feet into the air, burst into over 1,500 metallic shards, and destroy anything flying within 200 yards (182 meters) of the explosion.

159) Some members of the British Royal Family, along with some influential aristocrats, had links to the Nazis before WWII started. For example, Edward VIII, who had been king just before the war, admired Hitler greatly.

160) Japan attacked Pearl Harbor (in Hawaii) because America had imposed crippling sanctions on them. The sanctions were a result of the atrocities they had committed in China, and many other pacific territories, some of which were under American control at the time.

161) The term "axis powers" was coined when Benito Mussolini gave a speech right after Germany and Italy signed a treaty. In that speech, he stated that Europe and the whole world would revolve around "the axis of Rome and Berlin," meaning that those two cities would run the whole world.

162) When the Germans invaded the Soviet Union, they opened the largest land theater of war in the history of

the world. The German invasion was known as Operation Barbarossa. The operation finally failed partly because German fighters weren't used to harsh Russian winters.

163) Pearl Harbor is located more than 2,000 miles (3200 kilometers) away from Japan. Because of this distance, no one expected such a daring attack, and the harbor was left unguarded most of the time. The US Navy didn't have anti aircraft guns ready for such an event and wasn't able to retaliate.

164) Polish soldiers in Italy used a bear called Wojtek to transport ammunition. The bear was domesticated and trained to work in a circus, and got along with the soldiers quite well.

Wojtek the bear

165) When the allied air forces raided Germany during the night, all cities turned off their lights so that they would be less visible to the pilots. The German city of Constance, which is located near Germany's border with

Switzerland, was the only one that left its lights shining bright. Allied pilots didn't bomb the city of Constance because it was unclear where Switzerland ended and where Constance began. The allies didn't want to accidentally drop bombs on a neutral country.

166) It's believed that Hitler was taking a nap when news got to Berlin that the Allied forces had landed on Normandy. All of his men were apparently afraid to wake him up and give him the bad news because he often had angry outbursts when things weren't going his way.

167) Apart from London, other British cities that were targeted by German air raids included Swansea, Liverpool, Birmingham, and Bristol.

168) During WWII, America banned radio stations from receiving song requests from listeners. They feared that German spies could use song requests to send coded messages back and forth.

169) The Soviet Union was one of the first countries to have women fight on the frontlines in combat. This had to do with them embracing communism, which encouraged equality in the workplace as well as in the military. More than a million women served in the Red Army during WWII.

170) Many fascists fled Europe after WWII. They escaped through networks of secret organizations known as "ratlines", and they settled in South America, Australia, the Middle East, and Canada.

171) Finland switched sides during the war. When WWII

started, Finland was already at war with the Soviet Union, so they sought the help of the Germans to fight off the Soviets. However, after signing a peace treaty with the Soviets, Finland re-evaluated its position, and it switched sides to fight against the Germans.

172) Only 11% of the 2,800 Japanese Kamikaze pilots hit their targets in Pearl Harbor. The other 89% either didn't make it all the way, or they missed the targets they were aiming for, and instead hit the water.

173) Claus Von Stauffenberg, a German General who disliked Hitler's inhumane policies, tried to kill him using a suitcase bomb. Hitler survived with a scratch, and General Stauffenberg was executed.

174) During the war, America created special decks of playing cards that their servicemen carried into battle. When soldiers were captured (or trapped behind enemy lines), they could pour water over the cards, thus revealing maps and escape routes printed with invisible ink.

175) Fanta, the world-famous soft drink, was developed in Germany during WWII. The country couldn't get the ingredients required to manufacture Coca-Cola during the war (because of trade restrictions), so the soda company decided to make a similar soft drink with locally available ingredients; and that's how they came up with Fanta.

176) Apart from Jewish people, Romanise, ethnic Slavs, gay people, Jehovah's Witnesses, and people with communist leanings were also murdered or persecuted in Germany and Nazi-occupied territories.

177) Spain, Sweden, Switzerland, and Ireland were among the few countries that remained neutral throughout the duration of WWII.

178) Penicillin was a very valuable antibiotic during WWII, but its supply was scarce. To deal with the shortages, the army collected soldiers' urine and processed it to recycle penicillin.

179) A woman named Irena Sendler rescued over 2,500 Jewish children from the ghettos of Warsaw during WWII. She would take the children, give them new identities, and set them up with other families. She buried a jar containing proof of the real identities of the children in her backyard, hoping to reunite them with their parents after the war. However, most of the parents were killed in camps before the war ended, and the reunions never happened. Still, thousands of children were alive because of her brave actions.

180) Anne Frank is one of the most iconic figures of WWII. She was born in Frankfurt Germany to a Jewish family, but they fled the country shortly afterward because of rising anti-Semitic attitudes. Her family settled in Amsterdam and they were doing well until the Nazis invaded the Netherlands. Her family had to go into hiding for two years during the war. Throughout this period, Anne kept a diary, which has been very important for historians seeking to understand what it was like to be Jewish in Europe during WWII. Anne's family was captured by the Nazis, and she and her sister were sent to Bergen-Belsen Camp, where she died in 1945.

Anne Frank

181) 80% of all deaths in WWII occurred in just four countries: Russia, China, Germany, and Poland.

182) The allies (China, USA, Britain, the Soviet Union, and France) became the permanent members of the United Nations Security Council.

183) USA and Canada loaned a lot of money, supplies, and weaponry to Britain and the Soviet Union during WWII. After the war, the Soviet Union refused to pay its debt, while Britain slowly paid it off for the next fifty one years.

184) The Nazis had at least sixty eight camps where they detained civilians and POWs across Europe during WWII. They included main camps (mostly collection camps), labor camps, concentration camps, and extermination camps.

185) Some American soldiers started collecting the skulls of the Japanese soldiers they had killed. They took skulls and other body parts as trophies, and some would send

dried bones back home to their friends and families. The military leadership discouraged this practice, but it didn't do enough to stop it.

186) Between twelve and fourteen million ethnic Germans who were born in other countries around Europe were deported back to Germany after WWII ended. Many of them had never been to Germany before.

187) America and Britain used German POWs for slave labor. Forcing POWs to work as slaves was against the Geneva Convention, so to get around this, the POWs were paid extremely low wages.

188) The Germans and the Soviets both had "scorched earth" policies during WWII. Under these policies, when a territory was about to fall into the hands of opposing forces, the retreating army would burn buildings and farms, and destroy railways or any other infrastructure that the enemy might use.

Ruined Kiev (Ukraine)

189) America turned away possibly hundreds of thou-

sands of Jewish refugees throughout WWII. Similarly, Britain had in place immigration laws that were hard to navigate, so Jewish refugees had a difficult time getting into the country. The allies however, weren't totally aware of the horror that was going on in Nazi camps until the later years of the war.

190) After WWII, Germany lost a quarter of the territory it had before the war started. Its territories were taken by Poland and the Soviet Union. The allies split Germany into two states. East Germany, was put under the control of the Soviet Union, and West Germany was taken over by the Western Allies. Austria was also sanctioned by the allies after WWII. It was occupied by the victorious allies until 1955 when it became an independent state.

191) Germany's currency during WWII was known as the Reichsmark. It was originally introduced in 1924. When the Nazis took over, they changed its design to include the swastika and other Nazi symbols. The currency was discontinued in 1948, three years after the war.

20 Reichsmark paper

192) Although the bombing of civilian cities is considered a war crime today, there was no specific international humanitarian or customary law that prohibited the practice during WWII. The US bombed sixty seven civilian cities in Japan during the war and Germany, Britain, and most other powers did the same thing at different stages during the war.

193) The Universal Declaration of Human rights came in 1948, three years after the end of WWII, but it was a direct result of the war. It laid the groundwork for the end of colonialism around the world, and the civil rights movements that started within a decade after the war.

194) The atomic bombs dropped on Hiroshima and Nagasaki were developed under the Manhattan Project, a nuclear research and development project headed by Robert Oppenheimer. The project had several physics labs located in Manhattan, but the actual bombs were built in New Mexico, far away from any population centers. Americans dropped the first nuclear bomb in Hiroshima on August 6, 1945, and the second one in Nagasaki three days later.

195) Both the German and the Japanese military tested newly developed weapons on civilians before allowing them to be mass-produced and used on the battlefield.

196) When Japan invaded countries in East Asia, it termed them "The Greater East Asia Co-Prosperity Sphere." Japan wanted people in its Asian territories to think of it as a liberator that was freeing them from European colonialists. This worked in some places. However, public

opinion quickly turned against Japan after many in Asia learned about their brutal war tactics.

197) Germany economically exploited the countries it occupied during WWII. By the end of the war, the Nazis had collected 69.5 billion Reichsmarks (about $27.8 billion) from other European countries, including France, Denmark, Norway, Czechoslovakia, and other territories.

198) WWII led to the development of artificial harbors. Fleets had to be docked at strategic places, not just areas with natural harbors. Most of the early artificial harbors were set up along the English Channel.

199) The world's first programmable computers were designed for use during WWII. These included the Z3 computer, the ENIAC computer, and the Colossus.

200) Two-thirds of all munitions used by the allied forces in WWII were produced by the Americans. That included warplanes, warships, tanks, artillery, and land transportation equipment such as lorries.

201) Armies on both sides of the conflict had more mobility during WWII than they did during WWI. WWII tanks were faster, and they were the primary weapons on the battlefield, not just the support weapons. As WWII went on, new batches of tanks became better armoured, and their firepower improved significantly.

American M36 tank destroyers during Battle of the Bulge

202) The Soviets put captured Nazi soldiers in "Gulag" labor camps. The conditions in these camps were terrible. Prisoners were overworked, underfed, and there were numerous deaths.

203) Portable machine guns became popular during WWII. Before that, machine guns were bulky and each one had to be operated by a small team. However, during WWII the machine gun was redesigned to be compact enough so that it could be carried around and used by just one person.

204) The Allies were able to out-produce the Axis powers (when it came to manufacturing weapons and supplying food to their soldiers), not just because they had stronger economies back home, but also because they allowed women to join the workforce. In Nazi Germany, women weren't expected to work in industries, because they were encouraged to stay home and become "good mothers."

205) Instead of using codebooks as they had done in previous wars, various armies decided to design ciphering machines. The German "Enigma Machine" is the most well-known of these devices.

206) During WWII, unlike previous wars, airplanes could be used to airlift high-priority supplies, equipment, and even to transport servicemen. This was a great advancement because it allowed armies on both sides to get to the battlefront in the shortest time possible. This made it possible for armies to move very rapidly and conquer large territories in a matter of days.

207) After losing many ships to German submarines during WWI, Britain put a lot of resources into developing submarine defence technologies, which came in handy during WWII. They developed sonar (which was useful in detecting the positions of German submarines), and they perfected the use of convoys to protect their ships

208) The death rate in Japanese labour camps was at 27.1%, which was seven times higher than the death rate in Italian and German labor camps. The death rate was especially high for American POWs; 37% of all Americans captured by the Japanese died in labour camps.

209) As a result of the raid on Pearl Harbor (and similar raids in Taranto and the Coral Sea), it became clear that aircraft carriers were better investments than battleships because carriers were equipped to defend themselves against air attacks. America and its allies started developing carriers in place of battleships.

210) 80% of all males born in the Soviet Union in the year 1923 died during WWII. Most of these men were only sixteen or seventeen years old when the war started in 1939.

211) More Soviet soldiers and civilians died in the Battle of Stalingrad alone (the deadliest battle of the entire war) than American and British soldiers combined over the course of the entire war.

212) The US Air Corps lost more servicemen than the US Marine Corps during WWII. Those who served in the Air Corps had a 71% chance of dying. Many were shot down, including George H.W. Bush, who was rescued by the Navy and went on to become the 41st US President decades later.

213) German forces never attacked the US mainland, although they had bombers that were within the range of the US East Coast, particularly New York City. At first, Germany had hoped that America would stay out of the war. When America joined the war, they were mainly focused on fighting the Japanese at first, and the Germans tried to avoid putting themselves in America's crosshairs.

214) A Japanese fighter pilot named Hiroyoshi Nishizawa is credited with shooting down more than eighty American and Allied airplanes during WWII.

Hiroyoshi Nishizawa

215) In the lead up to the war, Hitler and the Nazis used posters, cartoons, and films to play on anti-Semitic sentiments in Germany, as groundwork for the holocaust that followed. One Nazi newspaper falsely claimed that Jews kidnapped and killed little German children because they needed the blood of Christian children for use during Jewish religious rituals.

216) Afghanistan remained neutral throughout the war, but it had close relationships with the three main Axis powers. In 1940, Afghanistan was banking on Germany winning the war; it made an official request to Germany to give it control over some more land in British India in the event that Germany won.

217) Due to international pressure to condemn the actions of the Nazis, some countries which had remained neutral throughout most of WWII (including Argentina and much

of South America) were forced to declare war on Germany just months before the whole war came to an end.

218) After the fall of France, its colonies in Africa (e.g. Algeria and Morocco) fell under the control of Nazi Germany. Vichy France (an unoccupied state in France that answered to Germany) oversaw most activities in these colonies until the allies retook the states after winning what came to be known as The Campaign for North Africa.

219) Australia declared war on Germany on the 3rd of September, 1939, because at the time, it was legally bound to be at war with any country upon which Britain declared war.

220) After Germany invaded Belgium, its colonies in Africa, especially Belgian-Congo, remained within the control of the allies. Congo was very valuable because it was rich in natural resources that were crucial for the war. The uranium used to make the nuclear bombs that were dropped in Japan was mostly sourced from mines in the Congo.

221) There were no battles in Antarctica during WWII, but it was the subject of serious competition between the Axis powers and the Allied powers. Even before the war broke out, Nazi Germany sent explorers to the continent, and it laid claim to large areas of the continent. During the war, the United States and Britain both set up bases in Antarctica so that they would have a permanent presence

there and keep Germany from claiming any more of the frozen continent.

222) In the lead up to WWII, Belgium declared that they would be neutral in the event that another war broke out in Europe. However, that only made them an easy mark for the Germans who invaded Belgium on their way to France.

223) Before the war, most islands in the Caribbean were under British control. However, since Britain needed weaponry it couldn't pay for, it made an agreement with the US. America would take British military bases in the Caribbean in exchange for several destroyers and other supplies. Even before America joined the war, it protected the Caribbean Islands and shipped tons of supplies from the Gulf of Mexico, through the Islands, and to North Africa and Europe.

224) At the beginning of WWII, China's army had 2.6 million soldiers. By the end of the war, the army had increased its numbers to 5.7 million soldiers. Throughout the war, the Chinese Army suffered a total of 3.2 million casualties.

Chinese soldiers poorly armed, snuggled close to the land for camouflage

225) Some European countries were totally defenceless when WWII broke out. Denmark, for example, tried to resist the German invasion on April 9, 1940, but were overwhelmed within just a few hours, and they let the Germans take over the country.

226) The city of Brazzaville in the Republic of Congo technically served as the capital of France between 1940 and 1943 during WWII. When Paris fell, the government of France went into exile, and it formed "Free France" outside the borders of the country. Free France, with the help of the allies, retained control of French colonies in Africa, and Brazzaville was chosen as the capital for the government in exile.

227) Indonesia gained independence as a result of WWII. Before the war, it was a colony of the Netherlands and it was called Dutch East Indies. During the war, in 1941,

Japan outfought the Dutch and allied troops and took control of Indonesia. Even as battles raged on in the Pacific, Indonesia remained under the control of Japan, until Japan surrendered at the end of the war. Five days after Japan surrendered, Indonesia declared its independence. The declaration was followed by the Indonesian National Revolution, and three years later, the country was totally free.

228) Emperor Haile Selassie of Ethiopia was kicked out of his country in 1936 by the Italians who wanted to colonize the country. He sought refuge in Britain, and he had been trying to get the allies to support him against the Italians. Luckily for him, when WWII broke out, his interests and those of the British Empire were aligned. Britain brought in troops from its African colonies, including Ghana, Kenya, Nigeria, and several other territories. The allies were able to retake Addis Ababa (the Ethiopian capital) in what came to be known as the East African Campaign.

229) Mahatma Gandhi was arrested by the British Government in India for leading a movement that called for India's independence during WWII. Britain heavily relied on the support of the Indian Empire (which included India, Pakistan, and Bangladesh), so they did everything they could to destroy Nationalist movements that were cropping up in the territory.

230) At the beginning of WWII, Iran was neutral, but Britain was worried that German nationals living in Iran had Nazi influence and they could potentially take control of Iran's oil fields. Britain, therefore, invaded Iran with the help of the soviets, kicked out the Shah (leader) and

replaced him with his son who was friendlier to the allies. As a result, Iran joined WWII on the side of the allies.

231) When Britain was recruiting fighters from Mandatory Palestine (what's now Israel and Palestine) for WWII, it made sure that it enlisted an equal number of Jewish and Arab soldiers. That way, after the war, no side would have a stronger army than the other, and peace could be maintained in the region.

232) Ireland was the only member of the British Commonwealth to remain neutral throughout WWII. Britain briefly considered invading Ireland to take over some of its ports for use during the war, but they decided against it. Germany did bomb the Irish City of Dublin because some private Irish citizens were aiding the allies.

233) Two and a half million Indian soldiers fought in WWII under British Command. India had the largest army raised through voluntary enlistment (other armies drafted most of their fighters).

Indian troops in Burma

234) Although Iran and the Soviet Union fought on the same side during WWII, the Soviets saw the war as an opportunity to take over control of some Iranian territories. They stirred up issues between the Iranian government and the Azerbaijani and Kurdish people, leading to both groups leaving Iran immediately after the war.

235) Iraq was the stage for a proxy war (smaller conflict) between Britain and Germany during WWII. Iraqi Prime Minister Nuri al-Said cooperated with the British, and as a result, he was overthrown by Rashid Ali who was backed by Germany. Britain then invaded Iraq and made the country declare war on Germany, but the Germans didn't recognize the war declaration because they didn't consider the British-controlled Iraqi government to be legitimate.

236) After the war, Switzerland was accused of helping the Nazis by allowing them to keep proceeds from the Holocaust in their banks.

237) Although Spain was neutral during the war, it mobilized a massive army to defend itself against invasion from both the allies and the Axis powers. As a result, both sides did their best to stay out of Spain because they didn't want another powerful enemy.

238) Japan occupied Korea during WWII, and after it surrendered, the Korean Peninsula was split into two. The north was occupied by the Soviets and the south by America. The conflict of ideas between the two superpowers led to the Korean War and the formation of North and South Korea.

239) The Jewish Community in Palestine was at odds with

Britain during WWII because Britain had restricted Jewish immigration to Palestine. However, the community saw Britain as their best ally when it came to saving fellow Jews in Nazi-controlled Europe, so they set their differences aside and joined forces during WWII.

240) General Douglas MacArthur commanded American troops in the Philippines during WWII. When Japan invaded the Philippines, he was ordered to move to Australia with other high ranking officials and leave his troops behind. He swore that he would return to the Philippines at any cost. He defended Australia for a while, as he rallied support for his plan to retake the Philippines. Two years after leaving the Philippines, he kept his promise and returned with more troops, and fought for the next ten months to free the country. Today, General MacArthur is considered one of the greatest and most inspirational military leaders in the history of America.

241) Hitler had a plan in place to invade Switzerland in 1940, but he decided that it would be a waste of resources. Switzerland had a fairly strong army and its mountainous landscape gave it a great advantage. Switzerland declared that it was on its own side during the war, and it actually shot down a few German aircraft for violating its airspace.

242) After Japan raided Pearl Harbor, between 110,000 and 120,000 Japanese-Americans were moved from their homes and into internment camps (forced relocation and incarceration in concentration camps). This was a violation of their basic rights, but America thought that it was necessary to root out Axis spies. Today, this is still one of

the most shameful acts performed by the US Government in modern times.

Pearl Harbor Attack

243) The Vatican was mostly silent during WWII. Vatican City (and the Holy See) had a treaty with Italy that required them to stay politically neutral, so they were bound to stay out of Mussolini's war business. Still, Pope Pius XII occasionally spoke out against racism throughout the war.

244) In the lead up to WWII, the Nazis introduced Nuremberg Laws which classified people into Aryans and Non-Aryans. The Aryans were considered a superior race, and the mixing of races was prohibited under the law. The Nazis also resolved to teach Germans to think of non-Aryans as sub-human.

245) The US Military was ready to put women in combat roles during WWII, but public opinion was generally against women serving in such positions. Women, there-

fore, only served in uniformed auxiliary roles. 350,000 American women volunteered for auxiliary service. They worked mostly as nurses, administrators, mechanics, drivers, and electricians. In the UK, women were drafted by the Department of Labour to join auxiliary services. Women in Canada formed the Women's Volunteer Service. Many women signed up from all over Canada. The service grew so large, and it was so well organized, that the Canadian government eventually decided to create the Canadian Women's Army Corps.

246) Britain was able to get more women into the workforce during WWII by promoting the idea of the "home front." The government made it clear that the home front was just as important as the battlefront, and if the home front was weak, Britain would lose at the battlefront.

247) During WWII, the US Government created over 200,000 different posters aimed at different groups in the country. The Office of War Information created posters targeting men, women, and people of color to join the war. They also created posters targeted at affluent people, asking them to buy war bonds.

248) In Nazi propaganda, Americans were represented as gangsters and cowardly murderers, just like Al Capone (who was world-famous at the time).

249) The US Government used radio programs to spread pro-war propaganda during WWII. President Roosevelt himself had "fireside chats" where he encouraged America to support the troops.

250) The US Government encouraged the creation of

"Victory Gardens" during WWII. People were urged to plant vegetable gardens in their backyards to help prevent food shortages. Through the media, the government asked women and children to plant these gardens as a patriotic duty, hence the name "Victory Gardens."

Plant a Vitory Garden poster

ALSO BY SCOTT MATTHEWS

Check out our most popular title: '3666 Interesting, Fun And Crazy Facts You Won't Believe Are True'. Search for it on Amazon to get your copy today!

Did you enjoy the book or learn something new? It really helps out small publishers like French Hacking if you could leave a quick review on Amazon so others in the community can also find the book!

BONUS: 3666 INTERESTING, FUN AND CRAZY FACTS YOU WON'T BELIEVE ARE TRUE

1) It is false that you can bite through a finger as easily as a carrot. It takes 200 newtons to bite through a raw carrot and 1485 newtons just to cause a fracture to a finger.

2) It took over 22 centuries to complete the Great Wall of China. It was built, rebuilt and extended by many imperial dynasties and kingdoms. The wall exceeds 12,000 miles (20,000km).

3) The largest empire the world has ever seen was the British Empire which covered almost a quarter of the planet in its peak in 1920.

4) Most of the camels in Saudi Arabia are imported from Australia.

5) China produces the most pollution in the world contributing 30% of all the countries total. These come from coal, oil and natural gases.

6) There are currently 1.6 billion live websites on the web

right now. However 99% of these sites you cannot access through Google and is known as the Deep Web.

7) Just like all languages, sign language has different accents based on country, age, ethnicity and whether the person is deaf or not.

8) There are over 1200 different species of bats in the world and contrary to popular belief none of them are blind. Bats can hunt in the dark using echolocation, which means they use echoes of self-produced sounds bouncing off objects to help them navigate.

9) When you're buried six feet down in soil and without a coffin, an average adult body normally takes eight to twelve years to decompose to a skeleton.

10) Pigs are physically incapable to look up into the sky.

11) The largest detonated bomb in the world was the Tsar Bomba on October 30 in 1961 by the Soviet Union. The blast was 3,000 times stronger than the bomb used on Hiroshima. The impact was enough to break windows 560 miles (900km) away.

12) The wars between Romans and Persians lasted about 721 years, the longest conflict in human history.

13) There were at least forty two known assassination plots against Hitler.

14) It took approximately 75 years for the telephone to reach 50 million users, the radio 38 years, 13 years for the television, 4 for the Internet, 2 for Facebook and only 19 days for Pokemon Go.

15) The biggest island is the world is Greenland as Australia is a continent.

16) In 2018, 4 billion people have access to the internet yet 844 million people still don't have access to clean water.

17) A single teaspoon of water has eight times more atoms than there are teaspoons full of water in the Atlantic Ocean.

18) Ancient Egyptians used headrests made of stone instead of pillows.

19) France was the first country to introduce the registration plate on August 14th 1893.

20) The Netherlands was the first country to legalise same sex marriage which was in 2001.

21) The average human attention span has almost halved since 2,000 decreasing from 20 seconds to 12 in 2018.

22) The oldest recorded tree in the world is reported to be 9,550 years old located in Dalarna, Sweden.

23) The oldest living system ever recorded is the Cyanobacterias, a type of bacteria that originated 2.8 billion years ago.

24) Being hungry causes serotonin levels to drop, causing a whirlwind of uncontrollable emotions including anxiety, stress and anger.

25) On Monday March 23, 2178, Pluto will complete its full orbit since its original discovery in 1930.

www.ingramcontent.com/pod-product-compliance
Lightning Source LLC
Chambersburg PA
CBHW071319080526
44587CB00018B/3280